Earth

Applewood Books
Carlisle, Massachusetts

978-1-4290-9413-9

To inquire about this edition
or to request a free copy
of our current catalog
featuring our best-selling books, write to:
Applewood Books
P.O. Box 27
Carlisle, MA 01741
For more complete listings,
visit us on the web at:
www.awb.com

10 9 8 7 6 5 4 3 2 1
MANUFACTURED IN THE UNITED STATES OF AMERICA

Earth anchors and nourishes life. It is, in many senses, the most stable of the elements. It is the place where seeds are sown, roots are protected and take hold, and life sprouts. It is no wonder that earth is such a potent symbol for home—personal, familial, cultural, and national. Our homes and homelands are the places that we connect with on the deepest levels, they are the places where our social and familial roots run deep, and they are the places that we ache for when we leave them. The inspirational quotations in this volume are a demonstration of the deep ties between land and identity.

Wendell Berry wrote that "the soil is the great connector of our lives, the source and destination of all." Soil—earth—is that living substance that makes food possible. Farmers and gardeners depend upon its health; we all do. And gardeners are quick to extol the beauty of life-giving, rich soil: "It was such a pleasure to sink one's hands into the warm earth, to feel at one's fingertips the possibilities of the new season" (Kate Morton, *The Forgotten Garden*). The literal touch of soil serves as a profound reminder of our human connection to earth.

—Applewood Books

"For all things come from earth, and all things end by becoming earth."

—Xenophanes, Greek philosopher

"No race can prosper till it learns that there is as much dignity in tilling a field as in writing a poem."

—Booker T. Washington

"To forget how to dig the earth and to tend the soil is to forget ourselves."

—Mahatma Gandhi

"If we surrendered to earth's intelligence we could rise up rooted, like trees."

—Rainer Maria Rilke

"Each soil has had its own history. Like a river,
a mountain, a forest, or any natural thing, its
present condition is due to the influence of many
things and events of the past."

—Charles Kellogg

"I saw all the people hustling early in the morning
to go into the factories and the stores and the
office buildings, to do their job, to get their check.
But ultimately it's not office buildings or jobs that
give us our checks. It's the soil. The soil is what
gives us the real income that supports us all."

—Ed Begley Jr.

"For what is life but a succession of change;
of one thing after another; painful beginnings,
fearful setting out into the unknown, leaving
what we are for what we have not yet become.
We sail forth boldly, keeping a steady keel and
a keen eye on the horizon, to reach islands, land
whose fragrance we sniff at the edge of our
dreams; and so we sail on, hoping that the next
landfall will be our own bit of earth."

—Suchen Christine Lim

"A soil is not a pile of dirt. It is a transformer, a body that organizes raw materials into tissue. These are the tissues that become the mother to all organic life."

—William Bryant Logan

"Oh beautiful for spacious skies
For amber waves of grain
For purple mountain majesties
Above the fruited plain!"

—Katharine Lee Bates

"Earth laughs in flowers."

—Ralph Waldo Emerson

"A garden to walk in and immensity to dream in—what more could he ask? A few flowers at his feet and above him the stars."

—Victor Hugo

"We must come to understand our past, our history, in terms of the soil and water and forests and grasses that have made it what it is."

—William Vogt

"Six years he had worked cultivating these beds, and hunting through the woods on the river banks, government land, the great Limberlost Swamp, and neglected corners of the earth for barks and roots. He occasionally made long trips across the country for rapidly diminishing plants he found in the woodland of men who did not care to bother with a few specimens, and many big beds of profitable herbs, extinct for miles around, now flourished on the banks of Loon Lake, in the marsh, and through the forest rising above."

—Gene Stratton-Porter

"The greater number of landscapes I explored, the more it seemed that they had traits in common and that the essence of each was not its uniqueness but its similarity to others."

—J. B. Jackson

"My hands will get dirty holding your rose-
shaped heart, because love is like gardening—it's
earthy and takes work to keep it alive."

—Jarod Kintz

"I believe that the great Creator has put ores and
oil on this Earth to give us a breathing spell…
as we exhaust them, we must be prepared to
fall back on our farms, which are God's true
storehouse. We can learn to synthesize materials
for every human need from things that grow."

—George Washington Carver

"Nature gives to every time and season some
beauties of its own."

—Charles Dickens

"Even with all our technology and the inventions
that make modern life so much easier than it once
was, it takes just one big natural disaster to wipe
all that away and remind us that, here on Earth,
we're still at the mercy of nature."

—Neil deGrasse Tyson

"They took all the trees
And put them in a tree museum
Then they charged the people
A dollar and a half just to see 'em

"Don't it always seem to go
That you don't know what you've got
Till it's gone
They paved paradise
Put up a parking lot."
　—Joni Mitchell

"Look deep into nature, and then you will
understand everything better."
　—Albert Einstein

"The fairest thing in nature, a flower, still has its
roots in earth and manure."
　—D. H. Lawrence

"At some point in life, the world's beauty
becomes enough."
　—Toni Morrison

"The warm sun kissed the earth
To consecrate thy birth,
And from his close embrace
Thy radiant face
Sprang into sight,
A blossoming delight."

 —Sarah Orne Jewett

"In every walk with nature one receives far more
than he seeks."

 —John Muir

"Plowed ground smells of earthworms and
empires."

 —Justin Isherwood, American farmer and author

"Land really is the best art."

 —Andy Warhol

"Service to others is the rent you pay for your
room here on earth."

 —Muhammad Ali

"Do you mean to tell me, Katie Scarlett O'Hara, that Tara, that land doesn't mean anything to you? Why, land is the only thing in the world worth workin' for, worth fightin' for, worth dyin' for, because it's the only thing that lasts."

— Gerald O'Hara (Scarlett's father) from *Gone with the Wind*

"Now I see the secret of the making of the best persons: It is to grow in the open air and to eat and sleep with the earth."

— Walt Whitman

"Buildings, too, are children of Earth and Sun."

— Frank Lloyd Wright

"As a single footstep will not make a path on the earth, so a single thought will not make a pathway in the mind. To make a deep physical path, we walk again and again. To make a deep mental path, we must think over and over the kind of thoughts we wish to dominate our lives."

— Henry David Thoreau

"[T]he great Searcher of human hearts is my witness, that I have no wish, which aspires beyond the humble and happy lot of living and dying a private citizen on my own farm."

—George Washington

"I preferred to plow without wearing shoes, and I remember vividly the caress of the soft, damp, and cool freshly turned earth on my feet."

—Jimmy Carter

"This land is your land, this land is my land
From California to the New York island
From the redwood forest
to the Gulf Stream waters
This land was made for you and me."

—Woody Guthrie

"Earth provides enough to satisfy every man's needs, but not every man's greed."

—Mahatma Gandhi

"Land, then, is not merely soil; it is a fountain of energy flowing through a circuit of soils, plants, and animals."

—Aldo Leopold

"This planet is not terra firma.
It is a delicate flower and it must be cared for.
It's lonely.
It's small.
It's isolated, and there is no resupply.
And we are mistreating it."

—Scott Carpenter

"Touch the earth, love the earth, honour the earth, her plains, her valleys, her hills, and her seas; rest your spirit in her solitary places."

—Henry Beston

"Earth, my dearest, oh believe me, you no longer need your springtimes to win me over… Unspeakably, I have belonged to you, from the flush."

—Rainer Maria Rilke

"It seemed that our family had been on this land
for thousands of years; that we had sprung from
the earth, born of its flesh like a tree or a flower,
deep-rooted, not by our feet, but by our hearts."

—Thea Halo

"There is nothing pleasanter than spading when
the ground is soft and damp."

—John Steinbeck

"And forget not that the earth delights to feel
your bare feet and the winds long to play with
your hair."

—Khalil Gibran

"There are no passengers on Spaceship Earth. We
are all crew."

—Marshall McLuhan

"Earth's crammed with heaven…
But only he who sees, takes off his shoes."

—Elizabeth Barrett Browning

"The environment is where we all meet; where all have a mutual interest; it is the one thing all of us share."

—Lady Bird Johnson

"We are all here on earth to help others; what on earth the others are here for I don't know."

—W. H. Auden

"What's the use of a fine house if you haven't got a tolerable planet to put it on?"

—Henry David Thoreau

"Those who contemplate the beauty of the earth find reserves of strength that will endure as long as life lasts."

—Rachel Carson

"'Heaven on Earth' is a choice you must make, not a place you must find."

—Dr. Wayne Dyer

"Today I have grown taller from walking with the trees."

—Karle Wilson Baker

"In all things of nature there is something of the marvelous."

—Aristotle

"It suddenly struck me that that tiny pea, pretty and blue, was the Earth. I put up my thumb and shut one eye, and my thumb blotted out the planet Earth. I didn't feel like a giant. I felt very, very small."

—Neil Armstrong

"The love of wilderness is more than a hunger for what is always beyond reach; it is also an expression of loyalty to the earth, the earth which bore us and sustains us, the only paradise we shall ever know, the only paradise we ever need, if only we had the eyes to see."

—Edward Abbey

"In seed time learn, in harvest teach, in winter enjoy."

—William Blake

"A garden should make you feel you've entered privileged space—a place not just set apart but reverberant—and it seems to me that, to achieve this, the gardener must put some kind of twist on the existing landscape, turn its prose into something nearer poetry."

—Michael Pollan

"The master of the garden is the one who waters it, trims the branches, plants the seeds, and pulls the weeds. If you merely stroll through the garden, you are but an acolyte."

—Vera Nazarian

"I had assumed that the Earth, the spirit of the Earth, noticed exceptions—those who wantonly damage it and those who do not. But the Earth is wise. It has given itself into the keeping of all, and all are therefore accountable."

—Alice Walker

"Take care how you place your moccasins upon the Earth, step with care, for the faces of the future generations are looking up from the Earth waiting their turn for life."

—Wilma Mankiller, Principal Chief of the Cherokee Nation

"In the spring, at the end of the day, you should smell like dirt."

—Margaret Atwood

"Earth Day achieved what I had hoped for and then some. The purpose of Earth Day was to get a nationwide demonstration of concern for the environment so large that it would shake the political establishment out of its lethargy and, finally, force this issue permanently into the political arena. Having criss-crossed the nation speaking on environmental issues during the previous eight or nine years it was clear to me that the public was far ahead of the politicians and given an opportunity they would demonstrate their interest…. An estimated twenty million people participated in peaceful demonstrations all across the country."

—Gaylord Nelson, founder of Earth Day

"The Earth is what we all have in common."

—Wendell Berry

"I would rather be tied to the soil as a serf…than be king of all these dead and destroyed."

—Homer

"Unless someone like you cares a whole awful lot, nothing is going to get better. It's not."

—Dr. Seuss' the Lorax

"To see a world in a grain of sand and a heaven in a wildflower. Hold infinity in the palm of your hand and eternity in an hour."

—William Blake

"Whoever could make two ears of corn or two blades of grass to grow upon a spot of ground where only one grew before, would deserve better of mankind, and do more essential service to his country than the whole race of politicians put together."

—Jonathan Swift

"God made a beauteous garden
With lovely flowers strown,
But one straight, narrow pathway
That was not overgrown.
And to this beauteous garden
He brought mankind to live,
And said "To you, my children,
These lovely flowers I give.
Prune ye my vines and fig trees,
With care my flowers tend,
But keep the pathway open
Your home is at the end."

—Robert Frost

"Mistress Mary always felt that however many years she lived she should never forget that first morning when her garden began to grow."

—Frances Hodgson Burnett, from *The Secret Garden*

"We spend our lives hurrying away from the real, as though it were deadly to us. 'It must be somewhere up there on the horizon,' we think. And all the time it is in the soil, right beneath our feet."

—William Bryant Logan

"A rainbow of soil is under our feet;
red as a barn and black as peat.
It's yellow as lemon and white as the snow;
bluish gray…so many colors below.
Hidden in darkness as thick as the night;
the only rainbow that can form without light.*
Dig you a pit, or bore you a hole,
you'll find enough colors to well rest your soul."
*(Direct light, that is.)

   —Francis D. Hole

"Wildness reminds us what it means to be
human, what we are connected to rather than
what we are separate from."

   —Terry Tempest Williams

"My garden is my most beautiful masterpiece."

   —Claude Monet

May your trails be crooked, winding, lonesome,
dangerous, leading to the most amazing view.
May your mountains rise into and above the
clouds."

   —Edward Abbey

"You might as well argue that because a tree is
planted deep down in Mother Earth, because it
comes in contact with clay, and rocks, and sand,
and water that through its graceful branches,
its beautiful leaves and its fragrant blossoms it
teaches no lesson of truth, beauty and divinity.
You cannot plant a tree in air, and have it live.
Try it. No matter how much we may praise its
proportions and enjoy its beauty, it dies unless its
roots and fibers touch and have their foundation
in Mother Earth. What is true of the tree is true of
a race."

—Booker T. Washington

"There is new life in the soil for every man. There
is healing in the trees for tired minds and for
our overburdened spirits, there is strength in the
hills, if only we will lift up our eyes. Remember
that nature is your great restorer."

—Calvin Coolidge

"While the farmer holds the title to the land,
actually it belongs to all the people because
civilization itself rests upon the soil."

—Thomas Jefferson

"We know more about the movement of celestial bodies than about the soil underfoot."

—Leonardo da Vinci

"There must be limits, somewhere, to the human footprint on this earth. When the whole world is reduced to nothing but human product, we will have lost the map that can show us how we got here, and can offer our spirits an answer when we ask why. Surely we are capable of declaring sacred some quarters that we dare not enter or possess."

—Barbara Kingsolver

"The land belongs to the future…that's the way it seems to me. How many names on the county clerk's plat will be there in fifty years? I might as well try to will the sunset over there to my brother's children. We come and go, but the land is always here. And the people who love it and understand it are the people who own it—for a little while."

—Willa Cather

"What a joy it is to feel the soft, springy earth
under my feet once more, to follow grassy roads
that lead to ferny brooks where I can bathe
my fingers in a cataract of rippling notes, or to
clamber over a stone wall into green fields that
tumble and roll and climb into riotous gladness!"

—Helen Keller

"I bequeath myself to the dirt, to grow from the
grass I love; if you want me again, look for me
under your boot-soles."

—Walt Whitman

"Trees are the Earth's endless effort to speak to
the listening heaven."

—Rabindranath Tagore

"We abuse land because we regard it as a
commodity belonging to us. When we see land as
a community to which we belong, we may begin
to use it with love and respect."

—Aldo Leopold

"To see the earth as it truly is, small and blue and beautiful in that eternal silence where it floats, is to see ourselves as riders on the earth together, brothers on that bright loveliness in the eternal cold—brothers who know now they are truly brothers."

—Archibald MacLeish

"It was such a pleasure to sink one's hands into the warm earth, to feel at one's fingertips the possibilities of the new season."

—Kate Morton

"For only rarely have we stood back and celebrated our soils as something beautiful, and perhaps even mysterious. For what other natural body, worldwide in its distribution, has so many interesting secrets to reveal to the patient observer?"

—Les Molloy

"Beautiful rocks—beautiful grass—Beautiful
soil where they both combine—Beautiful river—
covering sky—Never thought of possession, but
all this was mine."

—Bruce Cockburn from "A Dream Like Mine"

"Our songs travel the earth. We sing to one
another. Not a single note is ever lost and no
song is original. They all come from the same
place and go back to a time when only the stones
howled."

—Louise Erdrich

"When we contemplate the whole globe as
one great dewdrop, striped and dotted with
continents and islands, flying through space with
other stars all singing and shining together as
one, the whole universe appears as an infinite
storm of beauty."

—John Muir

"We have become great because of the lavish use of our resources…But the time has come to inquire seriously what will happen when our forests are gone, when the coal, the iron, the oil and the gas are exhausted."

—Theodore Roosevelt

"Something will have gone out of us as a people if we ever let the remaining wilderness be destroyed…so that never again can we have the chance to see ourselves single, separate, vertical and individual in the world, part of the environment of trees and rocks and soil, part of the natural world and competent to belong in it."

—Wallace Stegner

"The single greatest lesson the garden teaches is that our relationship to the planet need not be zero-sum, and that as long as the sun still shines and people still can plan and plant, think and do, we can, if we bother to try, find ways to provide for ourselves without diminishing the world."

—Michael Pollan

"It is my land, my home, my father's land, to
which I now ask to be allowed to return. I want
to spend my last days there, and be buried
among those mountains. If this could be I might
die in peace..."

  —Geronimo

"The nation that destroys its soil, destroys itself."

  —Franklin Delano Roosevelt

"For you little gardener and lover of trees, I have
only a small gift. Here is set G for Galadriel, but
it may stand for garden in your tongue. In this
box there is earth from my orchard, and such
blessing as Galadriel has still to bestow is upon it.
It will not keep you on your road, nor defend you
against any peril; but if you keep it and see your
home again at last, then perhaps it may reward
you. Though you should find all barren and laid
waste, there will be few gardens in Middle-earth
that will bloom like your garden, if you sprinkle
this earth there."

  —J. R. R. Tolkien

"Now I know a refuge never grows from a chin in a hand in a thoughtful pose; tend the earth if you want a rose."

—Emily Saliers from "Hammer and a Nail"

"People in cities may forget the soil for as long as a hundred years, but Mother Nature's memory is long and she will not let them forget indefinitely."

—Henry Cantwell Wallace

"Our kinship with Earth must be maintained; otherwise, we will find ourselves trapped in the center of our own paved-over souls with no way out."

—Terry Tempest Williams

"The soil of any one place makes its own peculiar and inevitable sense. It is impossible to contemplate the life of the soil for very long without seeing it as analogous to the life of the spirit."

—Wendell Berry

"I went to the woods because I wished to live deliberately, to front only the essential facts of life, and see if I could not learn what it had to teach, and not, when I came to die, discover that I had not lived."

—Henry David Thoreau

"A blade of grass is a commonplace on Earth; it would be a miracle on Mars. Our descendants on Mars will know the value of a patch of green. And if a blade of grass is priceless, what is the value of a human being?"

—Carl Sagan

"The mountains are fountains of men as well as of rivers, of glaciers, of fertile soil. The great poets, philosophers, prophets, able men whose thoughts and deeds have moved the world, have come down from the mountains—mountain-dwellers who have grown strong there with the forest trees in Nature's work-shops."

—John Muir

"We who are gathered here may represent a particular elite, not of money and power, but of concern for the earth for the earth's sake."

　—Ansel Adams

"Earth and sky, woods and fields, lakes and rivers, the mountain and the sea, are excellent schoolmasters, and teach some of us more than we can ever learn from books."

　—Sir John Lubbock

"The land, the earth God gave to man for his home…should never be the possession of any man, corporation, (or) society…any more than the air or water. Laws change; people die; the land remains."

　—Abraham Lincoln